WHY GOD BECAME MAN

by

P. B. FITZWATER, D.D.
Bible Teacher in the Moody Bible Institute,
Preacher, Author and Lecturer

Wipf & Stock
PUBLISHERS
Eugene, Oregon

Wipf and Stock Publishers
199 W 8th Ave, Suite 3
Eugene, OR 97401

Why God Became Man
By Fitzwater, P.B.

ISBN: 1-59752-145-0
Publication date 4/13/2005
Previously published by Moody Press, 1934

FOREWORD

The universe is Christocentric. All the plans and purposes of God as to men, angels, and the entire creation converge in Jesus Christ. Departure from this center has wrought all kinds of confusion in the thought and life of the world.

Those who grasp the stupendous truth of the incarnation of God in Christ will be consistent in their thinking both in the realm of science and theology. The hope of the world spiritually and materially is its unification in Christ. Universal peace can only come through universal harmony of thought and purpose. This in turn can only come as the mind and heart of the race gathers around and centers in the personality of Jesus Christ, the Word of God made flesh. As an aid to right thinking on this important subject, this brief treatise is offered to all earnest inquirers after truth.

By the incarnation is meant that in the person of Jesus Christ the eternal God embodied Himself and tabernacled among men; the divine and human natures interpenetrating, thereby becoming one. It was not the divine nature filling the human, as an empty vessel is filled, but the divine Person taking up within Himself the human nature, thus becoming the God-man.

"God was in Christ reconciling the world unto himself" (II Corinthians 5:19).

THE INCARNATION OF GOD IN CHRIST

OR THE

ETERNAL WORD MADE FLESH

"IN the beginning was the Word, and the Word was with God, and the Word was God. The same was in the beginning with God. All things were made by him; and without him was not any thing made that was made. In him was life; and the life was the light of men. And the light shineth in darkness; and the darkness comprehended it not. . . . . And the Word was made flesh, and dwelt among us, (and we beheld his glory, the glory as of the only begotten of the Father,) full of grace and truth." John 1:1-5, 14

CHAPTER I

THE INCARNATION BEFORE TIME
OR THE
ETERNAL PURPOSE OF THE INCARNATION

COLOSSIANS 1:14-19

"He is before all things"

Antedating creation was the eternal purpose of God conditioning all things which were to be as to their origin and end (Eph. 3:9-11). The incarnation was not an afterthought of God; not something grafted on creation because of the appearance of sin in the world. It was included in the original plan of the universe.

Ordinarily the incarnation of Christ is thought of as God's resourceful response to the exigency of sin, but the clear implications of Scripture are to the effect that creation and redemption are integral parts of a grand whole. Incarnation is absolutely essential to the redemption of the race from sin, but it extends in its implications and effects to the widest regions of the universe.

The Son of God incarnate is the connecting link, binding together God and creation. We thus see that the incarnation is the pivot on which everything in creation is made to turn. Christ was the Lamb slain from the foundation of the world (Rev. 13:8). Creation was made on lines of redemption. All things in the universe are ultimately to be gathered together in Christ as head (Eph. 1:10).

There are no contingencies in God's plan. Christ's relationship to the universe is vital and organic. His incarnation was in order that He might die as the world's Redeemer (Heb. 2:14); but it is more—it is the medium through which the whole universe is carried forward to its goal. Not only redeemed humanity, but all things in heaven and earth, are ultimately to be gathered together in Christ as head. He was the creative agent and final cause of the universe (Col. 1:16). A being less than God could not have done this, and a real humanity was the required connection.

These truths have been orderly set forth by Dr. James Orr substantially as follows:

> 1. The Scriptures know of only one undivided purpose of God—that eternal purpose which He purposed in Christ Jesus, and which embraces both creation and redemption.
>
> 2. We have the clearest acknowledgment, as has been already shown, of a direct relation of the Son to the work of creation (Eph. 3:9). It does not detract from the sugges-

tiveness of the Scripture passages which declare this relation, but immensely adds to it, that the Creator is at the same time the Redeemer. The implications of the Scripture passages bring into line the work of creation and the work of redemption, showing them to be parts of one divine plan.

3. Still more significant is the fact already insisted on, that in some of the passages (I Cor. 8:6; Col. 1:14-18) Christ is not only represented as the agent in creation, but the final cause of creation. He is Alpha and Omega, the first and the last (Rev. 1:8, 17).

4. Then there are the expressed statements already quoted of the goal to which God's purpose actually tends. This is further corroborated by the words of Bishop Lightfoot in commenting upon the phrase "unto him" in Colossians 1:16, R. V.:

"All things must find their meeting point, their reconciliation at length in Him from whom they took their rise—in the Word as mediatorial agent and through the Word in the Father as the primary source. This ultimate goal of the present dispensation in time is similarly stated in several passages. Sometimes it is represented as the birth-throe and deliverance of all creation through Christ (Rom. 8:19-23). Sometimes it is the absolute and final subjection of universal nature to Him (I Cor. 15:28). Sometimes it is the reconciliation of all things through Him (Col. 1:20). Sometimes it is the recapitulation,

> the gathering up in one head of the universe in Him (Eph. 1:10). The image involved in this last passage best illustrates the particular expression in the text, but all alike enunciate the same truth in different terms. The Eternal Word is the goal of the universe as He was the starting point. It must end in unity as it proceeded from unity; and the center of this unity is Christ."

This eternal purpose was foretold in the Old Testament. In pronouncing sentence upon the serpent, the Lord God said, "I will put enmity between thee and the woman, and between thy seed and her seed; it shall bruise thy head, and thou shalt bruise his heel." The coming Deliverer is here spoken of as the "seed of the woman." The crushing of the serpent's head is to be done by the seed of the woman. If the seed of the woman here meant an ordinary descendant of the first parents, it would have seemed proper to refer to the seed of Adam as the representative head.

In Genesis 12:1-3 the blessing which should come to all the families of the earth was to be in Abraham's seed. In Genesis 49:10 the promise is narrowed down to the tribe of Judah. In II Samuel 7:8-16 the expectation takes the form of a covenant which fixes the Deliverer to be David's son. A perpetual dynasty is thus established which shall become universal, bringing peace and blessing to the world.

The Messianic kingdom bulks quite large in the Psalms. The crowning sign is set forth in Isaiah 7:14. This Deliverer was to be called "Immanuel" while at the same time He was to be the son of a virgin. In Isaiah 9:6 and 7, the same birth is evidently set forth. In this case, the child which was to be born was to occupy David's throne. The One thus to occupy the Davidic throne was to bear these marvelous titles: Wonderful, Counsellor, The mighty God, The everlasting Father, and The Prince of Peace. Uniting these ideas, we find that the One whose kingdom was to be universal in extent was to be both human and divine. The eternal purpose is thus set forth to be fulfilled through this coming One who would be both divine and human.

CHAPTER II

THE INCARNATION IN TIME

OR THE

VIRGIN BIRTH OF CHRIST

MATTHEW 1:18-24

"They shall call his name Immanuel"

By the virgin birth is meant the historic fulfillment of the prophetic prediction concerning the advent of the divine-human, Redeemer-Deliverer. It concerns the identification of the Son of God as the Deliverer of the human race through His incorporation with it. In Luke 1:26-56 and Luke 2:4-7 is given the testimony of Mary, the virgin, who was to be the vehicle through which the Saviour was to come. In Matthew 1:18-25 we have the testimony of the angel of the Lord to Joseph, to whom Mary was betrothed. Their united testimony is to the effect that the birth of Jesus in Bethlehem was the fulfillment of the virgin prediction of Isaiah 7:14.

The respective genealogies of Matthew and Luke agree with their testimony. The apparent discrepancy between the two genealogies disappears when we consider that Luke is tracing Christ's genealogy through Mary, while Matthew is tracing it through Joseph. In Luke the genealogy is traced back to Adam, the head of the race, showing Christ to be the Redeemer of the human race, while in Matthew the genealogy is traced back to David and Abraham, showing Christ's legal right to occupy the throne of David as a descendant of Abraham. Since Matthew was concerned with the lawful King, His right to rule must be shown to rest upon His Davidic lineage through Joseph, His legal father.

These facts were likely communicated to Jesus by His mother. Humanly speaking, this may account for His divine consciousness when He called the temple His Father's house, and declared that He must be about His Father's business. The apostle John must have known this, because he declares that the Word was made flesh (John 1:14). By this term "flesh" he meant that the eternal personality designated the "Word" had united Himself to humanity. Paul clearly had knowledge of the virgin birth, for in Romans 1:3 the Saviour is presented as the seed of David, and in Galatians 4:4 He is declared to be the Son of God, sent forth by God, made of a woman, made under the law. This is evidently a fulfillment of Isaiah 7:14 and Genesis 3:15. It is because of this divine-human origin that Christ is called the Son of God. In the consideration of the incorporation of the Saviour with the race, let us observe:

I. The Act of Incarnation (Luke 1:35).

It should be constantly borne in mind that the virgin birth of Christ was not the origin of His personality, but the entrance of His personality into the conditions of human life. The divine person became human, and yet was none the less divine. We should note again that the only One in all history who could choose His mother, chose one in the middle stratum of society, making Him near to the rich as well as near to the poor. The manner of Christ's entrance into the world is a matter of great importance. No thoughtful person will be indifferent to this subject. Those who have faith in the integrity of Christ's person are greatly interested in the manner of His coming into the world.

1. The human nature of Christ was created by the Holy Spirit (Matthew 1:18, 20). Gabriel declared unto Mary, "The Holy Ghost shall come upon thee." Jesus Christ was not the child of Joseph and Mary as we are children of our parents. Jesus had no human father. His human nature originated miraculously in the humanity of His virgin mother by the creative power of the Holy Spirit. This fact explains why Jesus was without sin. He was a real man because He was born of a woman, and yet He was sinless because

He was conceived by the Holy Ghost. His incarnation was the beginning of a new humanity. Adam had no human father; he was created by God. Adam, as the first man, was the head of the race. So Jesus had no human father; His humanity was created. Jesus Christ as the second man is the head of a new race; He is the last Adam. Just as all the race was in Adam, its head, so all of the new race, the redeemed, are in Christ. This was included in the eternal purpose of God in creation.

2. The eternal Son of God united Himself with the human nature created by the Holy Spirit. The declaration, "the power of the Highest shall overshadow thee," does not refer to the creative act of the Holy Spirit, but refers to the act of the eternal Son who was overshadowing Mary while the Holy Spirit was creating the humanity which He was to take upon Him in vital union with Himself. It is because of this union that Jesus was to be called the Son of God. He was not the Son of God because He was born of Mary, for she was not the mother of God, as some falsely teach, but He was called the Son of God after humanity had become united to Him, because He was God's eternal Son.

II. The Fact of the Incarnation (John 1:14; compare I Timothy 1:15).

The Son of God was made flesh. Observe also that He "came into the world." His coming into the world shows that He did not originate here. Also He came in His own energy. He had a preëxistence. He came down from heaven (John 6:38). He came forth from the Father and came into the world (John 16:28). He came to be with men; therefore He became a man.

1. The Word was made flesh. The Word which was made flesh was the eternal Son of God, coexistent with the Father, a personal being who enjoyed fellowship with God. It was not Jesus, nor the Christ who was made flesh, but the eternal Word, the eternal Son.

2. He was made flesh, therefore He possessed a human nature. Just as He in His preëxistent state was God, in due time He became human. Because of the reality of His humanity, He became physically, mentally, morally, and emotionally Immanuel, God with us.

3. He became so perfectly man that He forever retains His two natures, divine and human. Just as He did not cease to be God when there was created for Him a human nature, so He will never cease to be what He at that time became. He did not put on humanity as a garment to be put off again. His humanity became an integral

part of Himself. He is now and forever the God-man.

4. In this union there is no confusion. Jesus Christ possesses two natures, but is one personality. There is no admixture of elements; both natures retain their essential characteristics. There was no formation of a third element differing from both. The union of the eternal Word with humanity brought together eternity and time. Upon this transcendent fact rests the philosophy of the incarnation.

III. The Purpose of the Incarnation (Hebrews 2:14).

1. To reveal God. "No man hath seen God at any time; the only begotten Son, which is in the bosom of the Father, he hath declared him" (John 1:18). The incarnation was God's point of contact with the race. Human nature was essential to reveal God to humans. We can only know God as He reveals Himself in terms of our own being. Those who ignore and reject Christ are absolutely destitute of any knowledge concerning the Fatherhood of God. The Unitarian who professes to know and worship God, while ignoring and rejecting the Son of God manifest in the flesh, is self-deceived. The representations in the Old Testament of God in terms of humanity only vaguely convey impressions to the human mind. The so-called anthropomorphisms

of Scripture should be considered as preintimations of the incarnation.

2. To bridge the chasm between God and man (Gen. 3:8). The rebellion of Adam's mind against God was sin. This sin created a chasm between God and Adam. Human history from Adam's time to the present bears witness to the reality of this chasm. "All have sinned and come short of the glory of God" (Rom. 3:23). "Behold, the Lord's hand is not shortened, that it cannot save; neither his ear heavy, that it cannot hear: but your iniquities have separated between you and your God, and your sins have hid his face from you, that he will not hear" (Isa. 59:1, 2).

Paul describes the heathen as "feeling after God" (Acts 17:27). Job realized his disadvantage as he exclaimed, "Oh that I knew where I might find him, that I might even come to his seat" (Job 23:3). He further argues his case by declaring, "He is not a man, as I am, that I should answer him, and we should come together in judgment. Neither is there any daysman betwixt us, that might lay his hand upon us both" (Job 9:32, 33). That need which Job realized has been supplied through the incarnation, "For there is one God, and one mediator between God and men, the man Christ Jesus" (I Tim. 2:5). The incarnation is the bridge which the eternal God threw across the chasm which sin had created between Himself and man, and over which man might pass into the arms of a righteous and yet forgiving Father.

Then, too, the incarnation is in harmony with the universal instincts of man. It necessarily lies in human consciousness. Max Mueller says, "There is no form of religion known to man in which there is no incarnation." Jesus, the incarnate Word, meets the universal human desire. All human philosophy and religion express the vain efforts of man to bridge the chasm between himself and God. All idolatry is but the effort of man to bring God in reach of his senses.

The genius of pagan philosophy is to bridge the chasm by various kinds of intermediaries, sometimes called emanations. It is said that in the philosophies of the people of India there are three hundred millions of incarnations. The incarnations conceived by the natural man are not only puerile, but are vulgar and positively wicked. The incarnation of God in Christ not only meets the needs of man, but is God's last Word which establishes a new and true philosophy, in contrast with the despairing philosophy of the heathen. The apostle John seized the "word" of Greek philosophers and declared that it no longer stood for an idea only, but for the divine expression of that idea in the God-man—"The Word was made flesh."

3. To lay hold upon man and save him (Luke

19:10). In order that the Saviour might lay hold upon man, He was obliged to be made in his likeness. "Forasmuch then as the children are partakers of flesh and blood, he also himself likewise took part of the same; that through death he might destroy him that had the power of death, that is, the devil . . . For verily he took not on him the nature of angels; but he took on him the seed of Abraham" (Heb. 2:14, 16). The incarnation is thus described as taking hold of the race. The force of this word "took" is pictorially represented in Matthew 14:31 where Jesus Christ, in response to the cry of sinking Peter, took hold of him and rescued him from death at the bottom of the sea. The incorporation of the Son of God with the race through incarnation was the reaching forth of the hand of the eternal God to rescue the race from eternal death.

4. To rescue the whole creation (Romans 8:19-22): "For the earnest expectation of the creature (creation) waiteth for the manifestation of the sons of God. For the creature (creation) was made subject to vanity, not willingly, but by reason of him who hath subjected the same in hope. Because the creature (creation) itself also shall be delivered from the bondage of corruption into the glorious liberty of the children of God. For we know that the whole creation groaneth and

travaileth in pain together until now."

Sin brought judgment, not only upon the human race, but upon the whole creation which was placed under the domination of the first man. Creation has been resting under the burden of that divine judgment ever since; yea, it is **groaning** under that burden. On every hand are heard its moanings. The animate and inanimate creation sounds forth its burden in the strains of a minor key. The incarnation of the Son of God is the divine method of ultimately delivering the entire creation from its burdens. All things in heaven and on earth are to be gathered together in Christ (Eph. 1:10).

Thus we see that the incarnation has:

1. A cosmic relation (Col. 1:16). All things created by Him—in Heaven and in earth—visible and invisible—thrones and dominions. Gather together in one all things in Christ (Eph. 1:10). By Him all things consist (Col. 1:17), atoms held together through the immanent God.

2. A soteriologic relation. Salvation only possible because of cosmic relation. Because of this the universe is preserved and life is imparted.

3. An eschatologic relation. The plan of God comprehends a goal. Attainment of a goal demands a dynamic. The immanent God through the incarnation assures the accomplishment of an end. God is moving forward to a fixed goal. His purpose cannot fail because He is linked with it. The truths of God's revelation agree with right philosophy and true science. The God of the Bible is the God of nature.

CHAPTER III

THE INCARNATION TESTED

OR THE

TEMPTATION OF JESUS CHRIST

MATTHEW 4:1-11

"Being forty days tempted of the devil"
(Luke 4:2).

Much misapprehension obtains as to the meaning of Christ's temptation in the wilderness. The prevailing impression among many Bible teachers is that it provides an example to Christians of how they can meet and overcome the temptations of the devil. Some one has said, "Under the irresistible influence of the Spirit, He turned aside to seek out in silence and alone the principles which should govern Him in His Messianic work." This implies that the thought of His being the Messiah was finally confirmed at His baptism, and that by His withdrawal into the wilderness He would have an opportunity to meditate upon and finally decide what was to be the character of His ministry, and thus He would come to know, in the midst of conflicting views, what His Messianic work was to be, and the course He would pursue. To this idea we cannot consent. In order, therefore, that a correct view of this temptation may be had, let us note:

I. The Purpose of the Temptation.

He was led by the Holy Spirit. It was thus unlike any temptation experienced by any other man. It was not a case of the devil leading Him into temptation, but of His being led by the Holy Spirit. It was not a preparation of Jesus Christ for His work, but rather His first conflict with the one whose destruction He had come to accomplish (Heb. 2:14; I John 3:8). It was not for the purpose of discovering if Christ would stand fast in the hour of temptation. It was not to see if He would sin. As Dr. I. M. Haldeman so clearly pointed out, this would make God guilty of setting up a scheme of redemption on the basis of a possible overthrow. It would also show that God's plan of redemption was unsettled until after the temptation. It would make it contingent upon a possible failure. It would further deny the absolute and unalterable decree of God. Antedating creation, God not only knew but determined all things which should be. "Known unto God are all his works from the beginning of the world" (Acts 15:18). These things could only be known because they were purposed.

Therefore, the temptation was rather to demonstrate the supreme fact that there was absolutely no sin in Christ, and that there was no possibility of failure on His part. It was to exhibit Him as an object upon which we may rest our faith with unshaken confidence. It proved that the humanity which the Holy Spirit created was inseparably united with the divine personality. The relation was indissoluble. The first man Adam failed. Christ is represented in the Scriptures as the second man, the last Adam (I Cor. 15:45, 47). He was thus demonstrated to be the head of a new race, the very source of its life. Thus it is seen that the temptation, instead of being a preparation of Christ for His ministry, was the opening battle of the dreadful conflict between Him and Satan. In this struggle, note in Matthew 4:1-11,

II. The Combatants (v. 1).

1. Jesus Christ.

As this was a Messianic temptation, the divine Man is seen to enter upon His mediatorial work. He went immediately from the place of anointing and heavenly recognition as the Son of God to meet the arch-enemy of the race.

2. The Devil.

Just as Jesus Christ was a real personal being, so the one with whom He struggled was a real personal being, filled with malice and cunning, and possessing great power. Those who deny the personality of the devil make the blasphemous charge that Christ's temptation came from within.

It makes His temptation to be a suggestion of His own imagination. In fact, it would show that Jesus Christ possessed a depraved nature.

III. The Battleground (v. 1).

It was in the wilderness of Judæa. The first man was tempted in a garden, with a most desirable companion and the most pleasant surroundings, and yet he failed. The second man was tempted in a barren wilderness, surrounded with wild beasts, and yet He gloriously triumphed.

IV. The Methods of Attack (vv. 2-9).

Since, as the Redeemer of mankind, Jesus Christ sustains a three-fold relationship, the Son of man, the Son of God, and the promised Messiah, each relationship was a ground of attack.

1. As the Son of Man (vv. 2-4).

This was a test of His humanity, to demonstrate the reality of the nature which He obtained through the virgin birth. The appeal was made to the instinct of hunger. Hunger is natural and sinless. Hunger is a sure sign of life. It is not the result of sin. Having been forty days and nights without food, as a normal man Jesus had a craving appetite. While the appetite was not sinful, to have satisfied it in a wrong way would have been sin.

The doing of a right thing in a wrong way is one of Satan's methods to cause many to fail. The slaying of the Egyptian by Moses and the bringing up of the ark to Jerusalem by David are two outstanding examples. Moses was conscious of his mission as the deliverer of God's people from bondage. No doubt this was taught him by his mother, who perceived from his infancy that he was a goodly child (Acts 7:20; Heb. 11:23). Moses' mother saw in him more than the average mother sees in her child. She saw him as "exceeding fair" which literally means "fair to God." Because this truth was instilled in his mind in his childhood days, he decided to suffer affliction with the people of God, rather than enjoy the pleasures of sin for a season (Heb. 11:25). The impulse of this conviction moved him to begin the work of delivering his people by slaying the Egyptian. He was mistaken as to the method and as to the time of the deliverance. David's effort to bring the ark to Jerusalem issued from a good motive, but his method was wrong. God had decreed that the ark should be borne by the Levites, and not hauled on a cart, even though it was a new one.

2. As the Son of God (vv. 5-7).

This was a test to prove that this personality which had united itself with humanity was divine.

The devil quoted from a Messianic Psalm to induce Jesus to presume upon God's care. He tempted Him to do the spectacular thing in order to secure publicity. It was a temptation to do a daring thing in order to get the attention of the people. God really does care for His own, but to ignore common prudence, or to do the uncalled for thing, just to put God's promises to a test, is presumptuous sin.

Satan today is thus tempting men. Undoubtedly, God has power to heal physical disease. As in the early days of the church, He can also bestow the power to speak with tongues. But seeking the power of divine healing, or the gift of tongues, may be only for self-advertisement. To neglect one's personal health, even in service for Christ, may be a sinful presumption.

This particular appeal to Jesus to cast Himself down from the pinnacle of the temple in the presence of the assembled throng, was to do a spectacular thing to convince the people of His Messiahship. If such had been done and the multitudes had beheld the miraculous deliverance, the presumption is that they would have accorded unto Him divine honor.

3. As the Messiah (vv. 8, 9).

The purpose of Jesus as the Messiah was to recover this world from the devil. The devil offered to surrender the world to Him on the simple condition that Jesus would bow to him, and thus obviate the necessity of His dying on the cross. The kingdoms of this world were in the possession of Satan, but he knew that eventually they would become the kingdom of Christ. The inducement he offered was for Christ to get immediate possession without the shame and suffering of the cross.

The same temptation is before us today, causing the Church to bid for power by worldly means. But the purpose of God from all eternity has been that victory should issue from Calvary. All who have forsaken the divine method of bringing peace to this world have yielded to the temptation of Satan. An outstanding example of this attempt in our day was the Interchurch World Movement, intended to achieve success in the wake of the League of Nations. The churches have not yet recovered from the effects of that gigantic blunder.

V. The Defense (vv. 4, 7, 10).

The instrument of defense was the Word of God. Jesus met the enemy each time and repulsed him with the words, "It is written." Each time He quoted from Deuteronomy, the book which the destructive critics attempt to discredit as unreliable. Jesus had enough confidence in it as the Word of God to use it as the sword of the Spirit in that crucial hour of the world's history.

VI. The Issue (v. 11).

The enemy was routed for the time being. Satan was not only vanquished, but the incarnation was proved to be most real. Thus it was demonstrated that the union of the divine and human natures was so vital that even the power of the devil could not break it. Because of this demonstration, man can confidently repose his faith in the incarnate Son of God as his Saviour. Christ did not come to show the sinner how to be saved, but He came to be the Saviour of sinners. Over the awful chasm between God and man, caused by sin, the incarnation formed the bridge which God provided, enabling sinful men to cross to the open arms of a forgiving Father.

CHAPTER IV

THE MORAL GLORY OF THE INCARNATION
OR THE
SINLESSNESS OF JESUS CHRIST

I PETER 2:22

"Who did no sin, neither was guile found in his mouth."

This is a doctrine which has not been given the proper emphasis during recent years. Vague impressions concerning it linger in the minds of most Christian people. Not only has it been neglected, but in some quarters it is positively discredited. The doctrine of the virgin birth of Christ and His sinlessness go together. Intelligent belief in the virgin birth is invariably accompanied with belief in the sinlessness of Jesus Christ. It should be borne in mind that Christ is a divine personality, embodied with humanity. His personality is the same now as before the act of His incarnation.

Some have sincerely misconstrued the statement in Hebrews 4:15, "But was in all points tempted like as we are, yet without sin." It should be borne in mind that "tempted" here is used in its primary sense meaning "tested" rather than solicited to do evil. This misconception is due to two things:

1. The assumed inability for Him to be touched by our infirmities unless He possessed a depraved nature. Let it be remembered that Christ's humanity was created by the Holy Ghost, and that it was because of this new relationship that He was designated "that holy thing." This holy being thus created was supernaturally preserved from the taint of sin, even though His mother was a member of a sinful race. In spite of His advent into the world through the channel of a mother who possessed a depraved nature, He was sinless.

Besides, the holiest men and women are the ones who most keenly perceive the reality of temptation in the sense of testing. It is entirely wrong to reason that only a drunkard can sympathize with the one who has become a slave to drink, or that only a fallen woman can properly sympathize with her sister who has lost her virtue. The truth is that because of the absolute sinlessness of Jesus Christ, He experienced real testing along every line, like as unto us. The notion that Jesus Christ had coursing through His veins streams of depravity, as in common to fallen man, is little short of blasphemy.

2. The failure to see that Jesus Christ is the Saviour of men, the personal object of faith, and not primarily a model for imitation. The work wrought by Jesus Christ was for human redemp-

tion, rather than racial betterment. Social up-lift is a by-product of His redemptive work. In fact, social up-lift is only possible because of the dynamic of salvation. Jesus Christ came to save lost men, rather than to show them how they could save themselves.

In view of these facts, both of these criticisms are unintelligent and dishonoring to the Son of God. The struggles of the pure and holy are far keener than those of coarser natures.

The sinlessness of Christ is proven by the following considerations:

I. The Reality of the Divine Personality.

Christ was free from both hereditary depravity and actual sin. The Scriptures present us with the portrait of an absolutely sinless man. In His childhood, youth and manhood, in His public and private life, He was without fault. Since He was a divine personality, and that personality had united with Himself the human nature which the Holy Ghost had created, sin was impossible.

II. The Implications of Scripture.

1. There is no record that Jesus Christ ever offered a sacrifice for sin, although He habitually attended the different places of worship. Since all the types of Scripture had their fulfillment in the antitype, and since He was the antitype, it would have been manifestly improper for Him to

have offered sacrifices for sin. The Scriptures are therefore in perfect harmony with the logic of the situation.

2. Christ never prayed for forgiveness for Himself, although He did pray for the forgiveness of others. From the cross He prayed, "Father, forgive them; for they know not what they do" (Luke 23:34). Knowing that He was inherently sinless, it would have been incongruous for Him to have asked the heavenly Father for forgiveness for Himself.

3. He challenged all men to convict Him of sin. "Which of you convinceth me of sin? And if I say the truth, why do ye not believe me?" (John 8:46). Into the face of those who violently hated Him and sought His destruction, He hurled this challenge. To this challenge there was no response. Even the devil himself was unable to bring a charge against Him.

III. The Scriptures Positively Declare Christ to be Without Sin.

1. "For he hath made him to be sin for us, who knew no sin; that we might be made the righteousness of God in Him" (II Cor. 5:21). It was the sinless Son of God who actually bore the sin of the world, and that gives potency to His atoning work.

2. "For such an high priest became us, who is holy, harmless, undefiled, separate from sinners, and made higher than the heavens" (Heb. 7:26). Three epithets are here applied to the Saviour: holy, guiltless, undefiled. This could not have been said of any one who in any respect bore the taint of sin.

3. "How much more shall the blood of Christ, who through the eternal Spirit offered himself without spot to God, purge your conscience from dead works to serve the living God?" (Heb. 9:14). Here the declaration is made that He offered Himself without spot to God. It is the spotless Lamb of God whose sacrifice is efficacious in the salvation of sinners.

4. "Forasmuch as ye know that ye were not redeemed with corruptible things, as silver and gold, from your vain conversation received by tradition from your fathers; but with the precious blood of Christ, as of a lamb without blemish and without spot" (I Peter 1:18, 19). Christ indeed was the Lamb slain from the foundation of the world, and it was because of His spotlessness and freedom from blemish that His sacrifice was acceptable as a substitute for the sinner.

5. "Who did no sin, neither was guile found in his mouth" (I Peter 2:22). Here again, He is declared to be without sin, because He had not

committed sin, neither was there ever any unreality in His life.

6. "And ye know that he was manifested to take away our sins; and in him is no sin" (I John 3:5). This declaration involves more than the committing of any sinful act. It asserts that there was no sin in Him. This could not be said of anyone who had either a hereditary taint or actual sin.

IV. The Testimony of His Enemies.

Two are mentioned:

1. Judas Iscariot.

"Then Judas, which had betrayed him, when he saw that he was condemned, repented himself, and brought again the thirty pieces of silver to the chief priests and elders, saying, I have sinned in that I have betrayed the innocent blood" (Matt. 27:3, 4). Though Judas was "a devil" and heartlessly betrayed the Lord, he was forced to confess the innocency of the Lord Jesus (John 6:70), and this he did after three or more years of a life of close intimacy with Him.

2. The Demons.

"Saying, let us alone; what have we to do with thee, thou Jesus of Nazareth? art thou come to destroy us? I know thee who thou art, the Holy One of God" (Mark 1:24). In spite of the sinful nature of demons, they were forced to acknowledge Christ as the Holy One of God. There is no disbelief on the part of demons as to the integrity of the person, work and character of Jesus Christ, nor as to the coming judgment. The reason that sinful men question and deny this important truth is due to the fact that their minds are blinded by the devil (II Cor. 4:4).

If Christ's human nature was not sinless then we must conclude:

(1) That He could not have been a Saviour, for He would have needed a Saviour just as any other child of Adam. It is unthinkable that a being with a sinful nature could be a Saviour of sinners.

(2) He could not have been properly called Immanuel. If He had had the slightest taint of sin, He could not have borne this title, for the One called Jesus Christ is "God with us."

(3) His death would have been utterly valueless as an atonement, for no one with a sinful nature could be a substitute for others in the same state. Judgment then would have fallen upon Him, as well as on the rest of the world.

CHAPTER V

THE UNVEILING OF THE INCARNATION

OR THE

TRANSFIGURATION OF CHRIST

II PETER 1:16-18

"Eyewitnesses of his majesty."

This transcendent scene is recorded in each of the Synoptic Gospels (Matthew 17:1-21; Mark 9:1-29; Luke 9:27-45).

I. The Occasion.

It took place shortly before Jesus went to the cross, following Peter's confession (Matt. 16:13-23). Christ's repeated announcement of His death, and His final rebuke of Peter for his unbelief, created a breach between Him and the disciples. There seemed to have been an estrangement on their part. This situation must be apprehended in order to grasp the meaning of the transfiguration.

II. The Purpose.

"And was transfigured before them" (Matt. 17:2). The purpose, therefore, of the unveiling was not for Himself, but for the disciples. At that crucial hour, they needed just that vision. If the disciples were to keep their faith through the dark hour just ahead of them, the light of the eternal must beam forth. In order to strengthen them for the ordeal through which they were about to pass, they must not only see the majesty of the divine personality, but must have a glimpse of the glory beyond the cross. They must see the ultimate triumph of Christ in the establishment of His kingdom.

III. His Mission Revealed.

"And, behold, there talked with him two men, which were Moses and Elias; who appeared in glory, and spake of his decease which he should accomplish at Jerusalem" (Luke 9:30, 31). Moses and Elijah, the two celestial visitors, were talking with Jesus concerning His exodus, that is, His decease or death, which He was about to accomplish at Jerusalem. It doubtless included also His resurrection and ascension. The very subject, which the disciples were unwilling to hear, was the supreme topic of conversation between Jesus and these heavenly visitors. The theme of their conversation was the thing of greatest importance. The supreme purpose of the incarnation was His death: "Forasmuch then as the children are partakers of flesh and blood, he also himself likewise took part of the same; that through death he might destroy him that had the power of death, that is, the devil; and deliver them who through fear of death were all their lifetime subject to bondage" (Heb. 2:14, 15). Christ's death was not accidental. It was not mainly moral and ethical, but dynamical.

While we do not know the full meaning of Christ's death, we do know that it is the expression of the dominant philosophy of the world. In the organic world the dominant law is life out of death: "Except a corn of wheat fall into the ground and die, it abideth alone" (John 12:24). The analogy of the organic world obtains in the spiritual world. Just as the seed planted must die in order that the new plant may come forth, so the death of Christ was necessary if any humans were to be saved.

While no one understands fully this fundamental law of organic life, all recognize its persistent reality. It is faith in this unchanging law that moves the farmer to sow his seed in expectation of a harvest. So constant has been this law through the centuries that suitable sustenance for living beings has been provided.

The operation of this law is as persistent and real in the spiritual world as in the organic world. It thus shows the necessity of the cross. If Christ had not died, He would have been eternally alone; not one human could have been saved. But in dying, the just for the unjust, and tasting death for every man, He is able to bring many sons unto glory "that he might be the firstborn among many brethren" (Rom. 8:29; Heb. 2:9-13). It is passing strange that this law, and the doctrine based upon it, should become so bitterly and persistently repudiated in these last days.

IV. The Person Unveiled.

To hearten the discouraged disciples, His deity flashed forth on the holy mount. The majestic personality was seen. In II Peter 1:16-18 we have an inspired commentary on the fundamental meaning of the transfiguration. Peter declares that the disciples were eyewitnesses of His majesty. The humanity created by the Holy Spirit veiled His deity. As He lived and ministered to others, He appeared to men as a man. There is no ground for believing that a halo surrounded His head. His humanity was real, but it was the veil of His majesty. The voice from heaven made known His character. He was declared to be the beloved Son in whom God was well pleased. In character He was perfect. It takes perfection to please God. When you want to know what pleases God, look at Jesus Christ. He is the ideal standard of perfection for all races, because He is the universal man. Our conception of perfection should not be a composite of the virtues of the best men of all the races, for in Christ we have the sum total of all virtues.

V. His Position.

When the veil was turned back and this majestic person was seen, He occupied a unique position, and sustained a definite relationship to certain persons who would be associated with Him in the establishment of the kingdom. The conception of the kingdom, which had vanished from the hopeless disciples, now gleamed forth. That the purpose of the transfiguration was perceived by the disciples is made clear by Peter's proposition to build three tabernacles. He may have recalled the typical significance of the feast of Tabernacles. This feast was an adumbration of the Messianic kingdom. Peter's proposition revealed the fact that he saw beyond the cross the manifestation of the Messianic kingdom. It was as if Peter said, "The millennium is come; let us celebrate by building three tabernacles." The unveiling of the incarnation is, therefore, the appearance of the kingdom in embryo.

The particulars standing out in this demonstration are:

1. The King Glorified on Mount Zion (Zech. 14:4-9).

As the disciples beheld Jesus in a glorified state on the mount, they looked forward to that time when Zechariah's prophecy should be fulfilled. Jesus Christ shall yet occupy the throne of His father David, according to the angel's word to Mary (Luke 1:32, 33).

2. Peter, James and John represented the Jewish Nation.

Christ indeed is the King of the Jews. The kingdom has been prepared from the foundation of the world for all who give Him loyal allegiance (Matt. 25:34). The King shall be surrounded by Israel in the flesh, together with all Gentile nations who are submissive. Jesus Christ is not the King of the church. The church now betrothed to Christ shall then be His bride, and shall reign with Him.

3. The glorified saints shall appear with Christ in His kingdom (I Thess. 4:13-18; II Thess. 1:10).

These glorified ones were represented:

(1) By Moses, the lawgiver, who died and yet was living. When Christ comes for His church, the dead in Christ shall be raised.

(2) Elijah, the prophet, represents the believers who do not die. The saints who are alive when Jesus comes shall be changed in a moment, in the twinkling of an eye (I Cor. 15:51, 52). They shall then be caught up in the clouds to meet the Lord in the air, and so shall they ever be with the Lord.

This truth has been the source of comfort for many of the saints.

4. Casting Out the Demon (Matt. 17:14-19).

The casting out of the demon, which had baffled the disciples, is an essential part of the transfiguration scene; in fact it is in this demonstration of the power of Christ that the climax is reached. The paramount purpose of the establishment of the Messianic kingdom is to destroy the rule of the devil. He shall be bound for a thousand years (Rev. 20:1-3). This act of Jesus at the foot of the mount shows Him as the King from heaven, taking possesson of the earth and freeing it from Satan's dominion.

The implications of the Scriptures are that as the consummation of the age approaches there will be unusual activity on the part of demons. They know that the hour of their doom is approaching. Even while Christ was on earth, they cried out, "Art thou come hither to torment us before the time?" But when He shall return the kingdoms of this world shall become the kingdom of our Lord, and of His Christ; and He shall reign for ever and ever (Rev. 11:15).

CHAPTER VI

THE HUMILIATION OF THE INCARNATION

OR THE

SHAME OF THE CROSS

PHILIPPIANS 2:8; HEBREWS 12:2

"He humbled himself, . . . endured the cross, despising the shame."

The Cross is a stumbling block to the natural man. Even among Christian leaders much confusion exists. Clearness as to the place of the Cross in the purpose of God is absolutely essential. Where this is lacking there exists no standard of thought.

I. The Fact of the Cross.

Matthew, Mark, Luke and John record the fact that Jesus was crucified with malefactors. Paul informs us that such a death was a curse: "Christ hath redeemed us from the curse of the law, being made a curse for us; for it is written, Cursed is every one that hangeth on a tree" (Gal. 3:13). The sinless Son of God was so identified with sinners in His death that He in fulfillment of prophecy (Isa. 53:12) died the death of a criminal. From Genesis to Revelation the Bible makes clear the necessity of a vicarious atonement. Just as the scarlet thread is found in every rope of the

British Navy to show its quality, so does the shedding of blood characterize the whole plan of redemption.

II. The Necessity of the Cross.

"And as Moses lifted up the serpent in the wilderness, even so must the Son of man be lifted up" (John 3:14). This necessity is shown by:

1. The Nature of God.

In His essential nature God is holy, sinless, absolutely just, and righteous. There is not the slightest flaw in His being. To entertain the thought of some imperfection in God is blasphemy. His nature as revealed in the Scriptures is in marked contrast with the reputed nature of the gods of the heathen. Because of the base conceptions they have of their gods, there is debauchery connected with their worship, such as puts to shame the practices of the underworld. The God of the Bible is just in His dealings with moral beings. His actions are always right.

It is because of this essential nature of God that judgment befell the Son of God when He took the place of the sinner. "All we like sheep have gone astray; we have turned every one to his own way; and the Lord hath laid on him the iniquity of us all" (Isa. 53:6). The words "laid on" literally mean "cause to strike upon," and show that the indescribable sufferings of Christ on the cross were the result of the reaction of God's holy nature toward sin. It was because Christ was made to be sin for us (II Cor. 5:21) that He suffered the agonies of the cross. Christ suffered in the stead of the sinner all that the sinner's sin deserved.

2. The Nature of Sin.

Sin is guilt which must be expiated, if the sinner is ever to come into the presence of God. Sin is uncleanness which must be removed before the sinner can enter into heaven. Sin is a disease which must be cured before there can be health of body, mind and spirit. Sin is not an abstraction, or something apart from a moral agent, but is vitally connected with the sinner. "Without shedding of blood is no remission" (Heb. 9:22).

3. The Nature of God's Law.

All men have sinned because all have disobeyed the holy law of God. The penalty of the broken law has to be enforced because the law must be upheld. Retribution is essential because sin cannot be condoned. If lawlessness should go unpunished, then God's government in all spheres would be repudiated. An atonement has to be made if God's justice is to be maintained. The doctrine of substitution is normal in a moral world.

III. The Method of the Cross.

God became universal man. Christ called Himself the Son of man. The blood of the whole human race coursed through His veins. Though born of a Jewish mother, He was the universal human. Because of this, He has a heart big enough to take in the members of all races, and arms long enough and strong enough to reach down to the depth of humanity and lift it to God.

When God laid upon Jesus Christ the sin of the world, He did not wreak vengeance upon an innocent substitute, but He endured the agony of Calvary (II Cor. 5:21; I Peter 1:18). God Himself provided the Lamb. Not only did He provide the Lamb, but the eternal Son Himself was the Lamb. This being true, the atonement of Jesus Christ in the highest degree is ethical. For an innocent one of His own volition to take the place of another, in suffering a penalty or in payment of a debt, has been recognized all through the ages as highly moral.

IV. The Issue of the Cross.

Christ was crucified with a malefactor on either side (John 19:16-18; Luke 23:32-43). This arrangement was not a happen-so. It parabolically portrays the different relationships of the whole world to sin and to God. It is the cross which causes a difference between men. By the use of the two prepositions "in" and "on" in connection with the occupants of the three crosses, this is made plain:

1. The Cross of the Unbelieving Thief.

(1) There was sin **in** him (Ps. 51:5). By virtue of the organic relation to the race, every human being is born a sinner.

(2) There was sin **on** him (Rom. 3:9). He was not responsible for the sin that was **in** him, because he was born that way, but there was sin **on** him because he yielded to his sinful nature. He was guilty because he railed on Jesus, instead of calling upon Him.

2. The Cross of Christ.

(1) There was no sin **in** Him (II Cor. 5:21). It is specifically declared that He knew no sin. Peter declares that Christ "did no sin, neither was guile found in His mouth" (I Peter 2:22).

(2) But sin was **on** Him. "All we like sheep have gone astray; we have turned every one to his own way; and the Lord hath laid **on** him the iniquity of us all" (Isa. 53:6). Sin was **on** Him as the divine substitute, and He bore the judgment which the whole race merited. His suffering on the cross was substitutionary and vicarious.

3. The Cross of the Believing Thief.

(1) There was sin **in** him. "Now then it is no more I that do it, but sin that dwelleth **in** me" (Rom. 7:17). By virtue of the organic connection to the race, even believers have sin **in** them. The holiest men and women have been the most keenly conscious of indwelling sin.

(2) But there was no sin **on** him. "Who shall lay any thing to the charge of God's elect? It is God that justifieth" (Rom. 8:23). Because the repentant thief believed in Christ as his sin bearer, the sin which he deserved to bear was placed on Him.

Each man has not only the power to choose under which cross he shall rest, but the solemn obligation rests upon him to decide it.

V. The Effect of the Cross.

The atonement of Jesus Christ in its outreach has:

1. Propitiated God.

Although none of us is able to fathom the depth of this truth, the Scriptures warrant us in believing that Christ's sacrifice has satisfied God.

2. It Expiated Sin.

There is such virtue in the sufferings of Christ that there is complete satisfaction provided for sin.

3. It Redeemed the Sinner.

By virtue of the divine arrangement, the vicarious atonement of Christ stands as a touchstone:

(1) To the sinner it means forgiveness of sins (Eph. 1:7).

(2) To the saint it means devotion to the will of God and the outpouring of self in service to man along the pathway which leads to the crowning day (Phil. 3:10-14).

(3) To the coming ages it will display the riches of divine grace and the manifold wisdom of God (Eph. 2:7; 3:10). The exceeding riches of God's grace is shown in the redemption of all kinds of men and women who were dead in trespasses and sins: "And you hath he quickened who were dead in trespasses and sins. Wherein in times past ye walked according to the course of this world, according to the prince of the power of the air, the spirit that now worketh in the children of disobedience: among whom also we all had our conversation in times past in the lusts of our flesh, fulfilling the desires of the flesh and

of the mind; and were by nature the children of wrath, even as others" (Eph. 2:1-3).

The manifold wisdom of God will be made known to the principalities and powers in the unification of all nationalities according to God's eternal purpose: "And to make all men see what is the fellowship of the mystery, which from the beginning of the world hath been hid in God, who created all things by Jesus Christ: to the intent that now unto the principalities and powers in heavenly places might be known by the church the manifold wisdom of God, according to the eternal purpose which he purposed in Christ Jesus our Lord" (Eph. 3:9-11).

The redemptive work wrought by Jesus Christ is much wider than the salvation of humans; it effects the whole creation: "For the earnest expectation of the creation waiteth for the revealing of the sons of God. For the creation was made subject to vanity, not willingly, but by reason of him who hath subjected the same in hope, because the creation itself also shall be delivered from the bondage of corruption into the liberty of the glory of the children of God. For we know that the whole creation groaneth and travaileth in pain together until now. And not only they, but ourselves also, which have the firstfruits of the Spirit, even we ourselves groan within ourselves, waiting for the adoption, to wit, the redemption of our body" (Rom. 8:19-23, R. V.). The deliverance of the whole creation will be manifested with the unveiling of the sons of God.

It should be borne in mind that Christ was the Lamb slain from the foundation of the world, and that He became incarnate in order that as a man He might die for men: "And having made peace through the blood of his cross, by him to reconcile all things unto himself: by him I say, whether they be things in earth or things in heaven" (Col. 1:20).

CHAPTER VII

THE DEMONSTRATION OF THE INCARNATION

OR THE

RESURRECTION OF CHRIST

ROMANS 1:4

"Declared to be the Son of God with power."

The resurrection of Christ is fundamental to Christianity. The word resurrection means "a rising again"—an "arising up of that which was buried." By the resurrection of Jesus Christ is meant the rising up—the literal coming forth of His body from the grave. The claim of Christianity for acceptance is based upon this wonderful fact.

The two elements of the gospel, which is the message of Christianity, are the death of Christ and His bodily resurrection (I Cor. 15:1-4). Christianity stands or falls upon this cardinal truth. If Christ did not rise from the dead, apostolic preaching is vain (I Cor. 15:14); the faith of the believers is emptied of its content—robbed of its object (v. 14); the apostles are false witnesses (v. 15); believers are yet in their sins (v. 17); and those who have fallen asleep in Christ are perished (v. 18). It is highly important, therefore, that every Christian witness should clearly apprehend the teaching of the Scriptures as to the resurrection of Christ.

I. Consider the Fact of His Resurrection.

There is no truth in all the scope of history better authenticated than Christ's resurrection. Observe:

1. Testimony of the Evangelists.

Matthew, Mark, Luke and John all testify to the fact of Christ's resurrection. These four men are not only credible witnesses, but their writings have been proven to be historically trustworthy.

2. Witnesses who at different times and under different circumstances saw Christ after He arose.

He remained forty days on the earth to prove the reality of His resurrection (Acts 1:3). He was seen of Peter, then of the twelve, after that He was seen by about five hundred brethren at once, the greater number of whom were living at the time of Paul's writing. After that, He was seen of James, then of all the apostles, and last of all by Paul himself (I Cor. 15:5-8). It is absolutely inconceivable that of this large number of witnesses there could have been any failure to set forth the truth.

3. Circumstantial Evidence.

The resurrection took place in the capital city, Jerusalem, and was known by the leaders of the nation, who were doing their utmost to destroy Christianity. Then, too, the apostles proclaimed this as one of the two cardinal truths of their message, in the same city and before these enemies, even charging them of murdering the Son of God, and that it was this Jesus whom they slew that God had raised up as a testimony against them. There was a transformation of the disciples from cowards, as Peter, who denied his Lord at the taunting of a Jewish maid, into bold preachers of the gospel.

II. What the Resurrection of Christ Guarantees Unto Us.

1. The Integrity of the Scriptures.

The Old Testament Scriptures tell of the advent, the death, and the resurrection of Christ. If Christ arose from the dead, the Scriptures are true (I Cor. 15:3, 4). It makes no difference what the unbelieving critics say about the Word of God, if the resurrection of Christ is a certainty. Happily, no event in all history is so well established. Christ rebuked the disciples on their way to Emmaus for their disbelief of the Scriptures concerning His resurrection (Luke 24:44-46).

Some one has counted the promise in the Bible, and claims that he has found nearly thirty thousand. These promises cover every human need, spiritual and temporal. Every crisis through which a Christian may be called upon to pass is included in their provisions. They pertain to the forgiveness of sins, prosperity and adversity, deliverance in times of temptation and trial during life, and even at the hour of death. It is the resurrection that gives divine assurance of the fulfilment of these promises. Were it not for the resurrection of Christ, all the promises of God would be as notes signed by a man who became bankrupt before their maturity.

These promises are like so many checks drawn upon God's exhaustless riches in glory over the signature of His Son. "My God shall supply all your need according to his riches in glory by Christ Jesus" (Phil. 4:19). If there be no resurrection of Christ then these promises are utterly worthless. "For all the promises of God in him are yea, and in him, Amen, unto the glory of God" (II Cor. 1:20). Therefore, we should read the Bible in the light of the resurrection of Christ.

2. The Reality of the Divine Person.

"And declared to be the Son of God with power, according to the spirit of holiness, by the resurrection from the dead" (Rom. 1:4). Jesus claimed to be one with the Father. He predicted His coming forth from the dead (Matt. 16:21; 17:23; 20:19). If Christ was not what He claimed to be, death could have held Him. But Christ declared that no one could take His life from Him; that He had power to lay down His life, and to take it again (John 10:15-18). He died because He chose to do so. His death was unlike that of any other being. The life which He laid down was necessarily resumed at the completion of His sacrificial work. His victory over death proved His divinity, and therefore the accomplishment of what He came to do. Then, too, if Christ be any other than God, as declared by His resurrection, His followers are idolaters.

3. The Sufficiency of Christ's Atoning Sacrifice.

All men are sinners and hopelessly lost. God's holy nature does not allow Him to condone sin, therefore an adequate sacrifice had to be provided. This was done in the person of Christ Himself. In obedience and suffering He met every demand of God's holy law. On the cross He declared, "It is finished." This meant that in His death the work which He had come into the world to accomplish was completed. It meant that God's full and complete provision for the redemption of the race had now been made.

In the resurrection of Christ, God declared

to the world that an adequate remedy for sin had been found. The living Christ at the right hand of the Majesty on high is the certification of God that salvation is possible to all who accept Christ. It requires a living Saviour to save; no dead saviour could possibly save. Men have hope only because they are freed from the guilt of sin through faith in a risen Christ (Acts 10:40-43).

4. The Needed Power for Life and Service.

"And what is the exceeding greatness of his power to us-ward who believe, according to the working of his mighty power, which he wrought in Christ, when he raised him from the dead, and set him at his own right hand in the heavenly places" (Eph. 1:19, 20). Every Christian worker is keenly conscious of his own weakness and the limitation of his power, as far as he is concerned; but he knows that the risen Christ has all power in heaven and earth, and that His power is available in his weakness. He should go about his work with confidence that there is nothing too hard for God and that "He is able to do exceeding abundantly" (Eph. 3:20).

5. Eternal Life and Immortality.

"Yet a little while, and the world seeth me no more; but ye see me: because I live, ye shall live also" (John 14:19). "Christ . . . . the first fruits of them that slept" (I Cor. 15:20). Belief in a life to come is universal, though somewhat vague at times. The guarantee that man, in the integrity of his being—body, soul and spirit, shall live again is furnished us in Christ's death and resurrection. In this assurance there is comfort for those who are in distress and sorrow (I Thess. 4:13-18).

6. The Certainty of a Judgment Day.

"Because he hath appointed a day, in the which he will judge the world in righteousness by that man whom he hath ordained; whereof he hath given assurance unto all men, in that he hath raised him from the dead" (Acts 17:31). As the failure of man to mete out justice is seen on every hand, thinking men sometimes question whether there is a day of divine reckoning. To all such, the resurrection of Christ should make certain that there is such a day of judgment when all acts of injustice will be adjudicated and all rewards will be bestowed. The resurrection of Jesus Christ leaves no doubt as to the ultimate issue of God's government.

CHAPTER VIII

THE PRESENT ACTIVITY OF THE INCARNATION

OR THE

HIGH PRIESTLY MINISTRY OF CHRIST

HEBREWS 4:14

"We have an Advocate with the Father" (I John 2:1, R. V.).

It was not enough that Jesus Christ appeared in the world, lived a perfect life, and died on the cross to make an atonement for sin. The Saviour needed by sinners is the resurrected and living One who can continue His activity on their behalf. Hopeless, indeed, would be our condition if we did not have His continued intercession. Ignorance concerning this ministry of the risen Christ has robbed many believers of confidence and peace, joy and hope.

I. The Present Activity of the Incarnate One.

"Seeing then that we have a great high priest, that is passed into the heavens, Jesus the Son of God, let us hold fast our profession" (Heb. 4:14). Thus it is seen that He is our great High Priest in heaven. The high priest on earth was taken from among men that he might represent them, even in their infirmities, before God (Heb. 5:1, 2). He was appointed by God to offer gifts and sacrifices on behalf of the people (Heb. 8:3, 4). He thus became the channel through whom God could deal with His people in forgiveness of their sins and the bestowal of gifts and blessings upon them. All this ministry is perfectly realized in Jesus Christ our heavenly High Priest. From the sacrificial cross and the empty tomb Christ passed through the heavens with His own blood into the Holy of holies, now to appear in the presence of God on behalf of His own.

II. Christ's Qualifications as a High Priest.

1. He is the very Son of God—the One of God's election.

"And no man taketh this honor unto himself, but he that is called of God, as was Aaron. So also Christ glorified not himself to be made an high priest; but he that said unto him, Thou art my Son, today have I begotten thee. As he saith also in another place, Thou art a priest forever after the order of Melchisedec" (Heb. 5:4-6). We are thus assured that our representative in heaven is the One of God's own choosing. Furthermore, He is the very Son of His love. Being both God's Son and the One of His personal choice, we know that His ministry is acceptable and efficacious.

2. His Office is Unending.

"Thou art a priest forever after the order of Melchisedec" (Heb. 5:6). It is not a question of the priest functioning temporarily and then ceasing to act, but the assurance of an unending ministry. The purpose of God is unchanging. Jesus Christ as our High Priest "ever liveth." Jesus Christ the same yesterday, and today, and forever (Heb. 13:8). "Who is made, not after the law of a carnal commandment, but after the power of an endless life" (Heb. 7:16).

3. He is Personally Sinless.

"For such an high priest became us, who is holy, harmless, undefiled, separate from sinners, and made higher than the heavens; who needeth not daily, as those high priests, to offer up sacrifice, first for his own sins, and then for the people's: for this he did once, when he offered up himself. For the law maketh men high priests which have infirmity; but the word of the oath, which was since the law, maketh the Son, who is consecrated for evermore" (Heb. 7:26-28). Christ being the sinless One needs not to make an offering for Himself, and because of His sinlessness He has a commanding influence before the throne of God.

4. He is Sympathetic.

"For verily he took not on him the nature of angels; but he took on him the seed of Abraham. Wherefore in all things it behooved him to be made like unto his brethren, that he might be a merciful and faithful high priest in things pertaining to God, to make reconciliation for the sins of the people. For in that he himself hath suffered being tempted, he is able to succour them that are tempted" (Heb. 2:16-18). Jesus Christ did not take upon Himself the nature of angels, but the nature of man, sin apart. Because of this, He can enter into the most definite realization of our needs.

As far as His humanity is concerned, He came into this life by the same door as do all men. He knows the temptations and trials of childhood. He knows the temptations and testings of youth, for He passed from childhood to youth. He knows the stress and strain of the adolescent period; therefore He is just the Saviour needed for childhood and youth.

He was a laborer and earned His bread by the sweat of His face, so He is able to sympathize with the great mass of mankind. He knew the trial of poverty, for He had nowhere to lay His head. He knew the temptation to be exalted which follows the sounding of praise by an enthusiastic populace. Because of this He can sustain men and women when honor is heaped upon them. He knows the trials of those who must meet fiery opposition, and therefore He is able to sympathize with and deliver those who are being persecuted (II Tim. 2:12). As He pursued His task, He became hungry and weary, so He can sustain all who are undergoing severe testings and bearing heavy burdens. He knows the names and the surroundings of all His own.

How wonderful it is that we have such a High Priest now in the heavens. There is indeed a Man in the glory who can and does sympathize with us. There is no place where earth's sorrows are more felt than up in heaven. There is no other place where earth's failures have such kindly judgment given. Christ is now most actively engaged in this ministry for us.

III. The Issues of Christ's Priestly Work.

"Wherefore he is able also to save them to the uttermost that come unto God by him, seeing he ever liveth to make intercession for them" (Heb. 7:25). Not only does He sympathize with His people, but He can and will save them to the uttermost. Although He is in the highest heavens, yet He is the omnipresent One. It is impossible for His people to be removed beyond the scope of His sympathy and help. He not only is omnipresent, but He is omnipotent. The devil is unable to wrench the believer from his Lord. Then, too, He is the omniscient One. Because of this, He cannot be taken by surprise. "For the eyes of the Lord run to and fro throughout the whole earth, to show himself strong in behalf of them whose heart is perfect toward him" (II Chron. 16:9).

1. He is in Heaven Preparing a Place for His Own.

"Let not your heart be troubled: ye believe in God, believe also in me. In my Father's house are many mansions: if it were not so, I would have told you. I go to prepare a place for you. And if I go and prepare a place for you, I will come again, and receive you unto myself; that where I am, there ye may be also" (John 14:1-3).

2. He now Appears Before God for His Own.

"For Christ is not entered into the holy places made with hands, which are the figures of the true; but into heaven itself, now to appear in the presence of God for us" (Heb. 9:24). Since day and night He is attending to His mediatorial work, He is able to completely save the believer, even though he may fall into sin (I John 2:1). Upon the perception and confession of sin by the believer, Christ the High Priest presents the merits of the perfect sacrifice which He made once for all in his behalf, and he therefore experiences the forgiveness and cleansing from all sin (I John 1:9).

Not a day should end for the Christian without the consciousness of full forgiveness and cleansing. Because the believer has such a wonderful Saviour, he ought to sing praises to His holy name continually. How can those who have this knowledge refrain from it! Salvation depends entirely upon the ministry of the High Priest He is a faithful High Priest. He never ceases His activity on behalf of His own.

CHAPTER IX

THE CONSUMMATION OF THE INCARNATION

OR THE

SECOND COMING OF CHRIST

MATTHEW 24:14

"Surely I come quickly . . . Even so, come, Lord Jesus" (Rev. 22:20).

Christ declared that the "gospel of the kingdom shall be preached in all the world for a witness unto all nations; and then shall the end come. . . . . And they shall see the Son of man coming in the clouds of heaven with power and great glory" (Matt. 24:14, 30).

The purpose of God in the incorporation of His Son with the human race by means of the incarnation logically demands His return to the earth to complete the work which He came to perform. The mediatorial work undertaken by the Son of God in conformity with the eternal covenant, embraces three definite functions, as set forth in the Scriptures.

1. His Message as a Prophet.

He came as the mouthpiece of God to make known the divine purpose. The ministries of all the Old Testament prophets were only meaningful as they looked forward to the final speaking of God through His Son (Heb. 1:1). All His servants and witnesses who have followed Him have continued this prophetic ministry.

2. His Ministry as a Priest.

On the cross of Calvary, the spotless Lamb of God offered Himself for the sin of the world. When He had thus offered Himself and cried, "It is finished," He entered into heaven with His own precious blood on behalf of His people. As set forth in Chapter VIII, He is now tenderly and effectively carrying on this priestly ministry.

3. His Work as a King.

When the purpose of God shall have been fulfilled in gathering out a people for His name (Acts 15:14), Christ shall return in person and power to establish His kingdom on the earth. This kingdom shall come into realization when He shall sit upon the throne of His father David (Luke 1:32). The completion of the work which the Father entrusted to Him requires the personal return of Jesus Christ to the earth.

I. The Certainty of the Second Coming of Christ.

In addition to the logical necessity, the certainty of His coming is established by a threefold testimony:

1. The Saying of the Angels.

"And while they looked steadfastly toward heaven as he went up, behold, two men stood by them in white apparel; which also said, Ye men of Galilee, why stand ye gazing up into heaven? this same Jesus, which is taken up from you into heaven, shall so come in like manner as ye have seen him go into heaven" (Acts 1:10, 11). All through the centuries, these heavenly messengers have made known the purposes of God. Many instances can be cited where things took place just as they announced. On this basis we know that these celestial beings can be believed.

2. The Testimony of Paul.

"For the Lord himself shall descend from heaven with a shout, with the voice of the archangel, and with the trump of God: and the dead in Christ shall rise first; then we which are alive and remain shall be caught up together with them in the clouds, to meet the Lord in the air: and so shall we ever be with the Lord" (I Thess. 4:16, 17). Paul had received a special revelation of this matter, as he declares in verse 15 of this chapter. Paul's life and ministry are unfailing credentials to the dependability of his testimony.

3. The Testimony of Jesus Christ Himself.

He said, "If I go and prepare a place for you,

I will come again, and receive you unto myself" (John 14:1-3). Christ's words have never failed. His testimony abides unchallenged. The believer has His sure promise, and can afford to rest upon that alone.

In these citations, the testimony of three witnesses is given. The Bible requirement, as well as that recognized by the courts of the world, is that in the mouth of two or three witnesses every word shall be established (Matt. 18:16).

II. The Nature of His Second Coming.

From the testimony above cited, it is established beyond peradventure that His coming is a personal, bodily one. The angels declared: "This same Jesus, which is taken up from you into heaven, shall so come in like manner as ye have seen him go into heaven" (Acts 1:11). The disciples saw Jesus ascend into heaven with a body, a body palpable to the eye. The declaration is that He is coming in like manner as He went away. Then Paul declares that the Lord Himself shall descend from heaven. It will not be the descent of another, but that of the Lord Himself. For some strange reason the conception of Christ's personal, bodily return has been obscured by the following erroneous notions:

1. The Gradual Spread of the Gospel and Ultimate Triumph of the Church.

This erroneous teaching is that by means of world-wide evangelization the people of the world shall come to a knowledge of Jesus Christ and recognize Him as the Saviour of the world. This cannot be so, because Jesus Christ Himself said that as it was in the days of Noah, so shall it be when He comes again (Matt. 24:37; Luke 17:26). In the days of Noah the people lived thoughtless and careless lives. They pursued their vocations and indulged in carnal pleasures, disregarding the warnings of impending doom sounded forth by Noah, the preacher of righteousness. This is a graphic picture of this wine-bibbing, gluttonous and pleasure-mad generation. Paul says that in the last days there will be a falling away from the faith, and that perilous times shall come. Men shall be lovers of pleasures more than lovers of God. They shall have a form of godliness, but deny the power thereof (II Tim. 3:1-5).

The parables in the thirteenth chapter of Matthew reveal the mixture of affairs in the world during Christ's absence, and absolutely preclude this idea of world betterment. Then Daniel's interpretation of Nebuchadnezzar's dream makes it quite clear that the kingdom of heaven shall be established suddenly by the smiting action of a Stone hewn out of a mountain without hands, and the pulverizing of the worldly kingdoms, to be followed in turn by the establishment of the Messianic kingdom (Dan. 2:34-45).

2. The Unlawful Spiritualizing of Certain Scriptures.

(1) They claim that the coming of Christ was fulfilled in the descent of the Holy Spirit at Pentecost (Acts 2). At Pentecost there was the descent of the Holy Spirit, but not the coming of the risen Man, Christ Jesus. He declared that it was needful that He go away, so that the Holy Spirit could come. He promised to send the Spirit following His departure from the world. In fact, He told the disciples that the Holy Spirit would not come, unless He first went away (John 16:7).

Furthermore, the mighty events predicted to occur in connection with the coming of Christ were not fulfilled at Pentecost; and it is still more obvious that this position cannot be true, because all of the New Testament Epistles and the book of The Revelation were written after Pentecost, and throughout these writings the coming of the Lord has a most prominent place, and is regarded as an event still future.

(2) They further claim that the conversion of the sinner means the coming of Christ. This cannot be true, because in the conversion of a sinner it is the sinner coming to Christ, drawn

by the Holy Ghost, and not Christ coming to the sinner. Certainly not one of the events associated with the coming of the Lord had its fulfillment in the conversion of a sinner from that day to this.

(3) It is also claimed that the death of the Christian is the coming of Christ. This is a fanciful interpretation which has gained wide currency without a shadow of evidence to support it. At death, the Christian goes to be with the Lord. "For I am in a strait betwixt two," wrote the apostle Paul, "having a desire to depart, and to be with Christ; which is far better" (Phil. 1:23). Then, too, the death of the Christian is designated by Paul as a departure: "For I am now ready to be offered, and the time of my departure is at hand. I have fought a good fight, I have finished my course, I have kept the faith: henceforth there is laid up for me a crown of righteousness, which the Lord, the righteous judge, shall give me at that day: and not to me only, but unto all of them also that love his appearing" (II Tim. 4:6-8). The word "departure" is a nautical term, and signifies a vessel lifting its anchor and spreading its sails, as it takes its departure from the port.

(4) Last of all, they claim that the destruction of Jerusalem meant the coming of Christ.

This error is very common, because some earnest students of the Word are confused, inasmuch as the destruction of Jerusalem and the second coming of Christ are so closely related in the narrative (Matt. 24:1-13). The careful study of this passage reveals the separateness of the events, and discloses the fact that the destruction of Jerusalem in a real sense is an adumbration of the great tribulation just prior to the second coming of Christ as the mighty conqueror. Only by the wildest flight of the imagination can the events connected with the destruction of Jerusalem by the Romans in A. D. 70 be made the fulfillment of the startling events connected with the coming of Christ in glory and power.

III. The Time of His Coming.

Christ declared that the disciples knew not what hour their Lord would come (Matt. 24:42). Nobody knows just when Christ will come, but it will be suddenly and unexpectedly. "Watch ye therefore: for ye know not when the master of the house cometh, at even, or at midnight, or at the cockcrowing, or in the morning: lest coming suddenly he find you sleeping" (Mark 13: 35, 36). The fact that the time of the Lord's coming is not known should not be allowed to dim its certainty.

IV. The Practical Bearing of This Truth Upon the Lives of Believers.

This precious doctrine is not theoretical, but is of the most practical value. It stands out in the New Testament as a lofty mountain peak overlooking the landscape. Every line of practical teaching looks toward, and terminates in, the coming of the Lord. The following examples are cited as instances:

1. Watchfulness.

"Watch therefore: for ye know not what hour your Lord doth come" (Matt. 24:42).

2. Self-denial.

"For the grace of God that bringeth salvation hath appeared to all men, teaching us that, denying ungodliness and wordly lusts, we should live soberly, righteously, and godly, in this present world; looking for that blessed hope, and the glorious appearing of the great God and our Saviour Jesus Christ" (Titus 2:11-13).

3. The Cure of Idolatry.

"For they themselves shew of us what manner of entering in we had unto you, and how ye turned to God from idols to serve the living and true God; and to wait for his Son from heaven, whom he raised from the dead, even Jesus, which delivered us from the wrath to come" (I Thess. 1:9, 10).

4. Fidelity in Service.

"Occupy till I come" (Luke 19:13).

5. Ministerial Fidelity.

"I charge thee therefore before God, and the Lord Jesus Christ, who shall judge the quick and the dead at his appearing and his kingdom; preach the word; be instant in season, out of season; reprove, rebuke, exhort with all long-suffering and doctrine" (II Tim. 4:1, 2). If the doctrine of the Lord's imminent return had been kept alive in the minds of the ministers of the Christian church, there would not have come the present apostasy. The realization that at the coming of the Lord, the minister must render an account for his ministry, and at that time it will be either reward or loss (I Cor. 3:10-15), would bring a sense of sober reality to those who are occupying positions as ministers.

6. It Gives Meaning to the Communion Service.

"For as often as ye eat this bread, and drink this cup, ye do shew the Lord's death till he come" (I Cor. 11:26). The communion service memorializes the sacrificial death of Jesus Christ for sin, and at the same time typifies the coming of Christ to complete His work of redemption. It is most stimulating, while surrounding the Lord's table, to realize that such a service may gloriously terminate in the rapture of believers.

7. It is the Secret of Purity of Life.

"Beloved, now are we the sons of God, and it doth not yet appear what we shall be: but we know that, when he shall appear, we shall be like him; for we shall see him as he is. And every man that hath this hope in him purifieth himself, even as he is pure" (I John 3:2, 3). The sure cure for coarse, vulgar and unholy living is a strong conviction concerning the imminency of the return of Jesus Christ.

V. The Results of Christ's Coming.

It is to be indeed a consummation. "Christ the firstfruits; afterward they that are Christ's at his coming. Then cometh the end" (I Cor. 15:23, 24).

1. Believers Caught Up into Glory.

"For the Lord himself shall descend from heaven with a shout, with the voice of the archangel, and with the trump of God; and the dead in Christ shall rise first: then we which are alive and remain shall be caught up together with them in the clouds, to meet the Lord in the air: and so shall we ever be with the Lord" (I Thess. 4:16, 17).

(1) The dead in Christ shall be raised first. At death, the Christian goes to be with the Lord (Phil. 1:23). The place of the believer between death and the resurrection of his body is with

the Lord. When Christ returns He will bring these persons with Him, and then the redeemed personality will enter the resurrected body and inhabit it forever. Paul was given a special revelation to disclose this truth. No wonder he says, "Comfort one another with these words." This is a real comfort which comes to the broken-hearted believer, who sorrows over the loss of loved ones.

(2) Living believers will be caught up with the resurrected ones to meet the Lord in the air (v. 17). At this time will come the change which shall take place "in the twinkling of an eye, at the last trump" (I Cor. 15:52). Paul declares that the dead will be first resurrected, and that the living believers shall be changed, and that both the dead and the living shall be caught up together to meet the Lord in the air.

2. The Marriage Supper of the Lamb.

"Let us be glad and rejoice, and give honor to him: for the marriage of the Lamb is come, and his wife hath made herself ready. And to her was granted that she should be arrayed in fine linen, clean and white: for the fine linen is the righteousness of saints. And he saith unto me, Write, Blessed are they which are called unto the marriage supper of the Lamb" (Rev. 19:7-9). Believers do not now constitute the bride of

Christ, but are His betrothed (II Cor. 11:2; Eph. 5:27). The marriage contract has been made, but shall not be consummated until Christ comes.

This is required for the completion of Christ's redemptive work. Then the hope of the Church will be realized.

3. Creation Delivered from Bondage.

"For the earnest expectation of the creation waiteth for the revealing of the sons of God. For the creation was subjected to vanity, not of its own will, but by reason of him who subjected it, in hope that the creation itself also shall be delivered from the bondage of corruption into the liberty of the glory of the children of God. For we know that the whole creation groaneth and and travaileth in pain together until now. And not only so, but ourselves also, who have the first-fruits of the Spirit, even we ourselves groan within ourselves, waiting for our adoption, to wit, the redemption of our body" (Rom. 8:19-23, R. V.).

The incarnation, as set forth at the beginning of this book, has a wider sweep than the redemption of mankind. Christ not only became the Head of the Church, but the Head of all creation. The deliverance of the whole creation from its bondage caused by sin is closely connected with the completion of the salvation of believers. The whole creation is now groaning under its burdens.

The whole creation has the minor key as its dominant note. This is because of sin. But when redemption shall have been completed, the major key will be the dominant note of the whole universe.

4. Judgment and Destruction to Those Who Know Not God.

"And to you who are troubled rest with us, when the Lord Jesus shall be revealed from heaven with his mighty angels, in flaming fire taking vengeance on them that know not God, and that obey not the gospel of our Lord Jesus Christ" (II Thess. 1:7, 8). Those who will not receive Jesus Christ as Lord and Saviour, but despise His grace by rejecting His gospel, shall meet their doom at His coming. They "shall be punished with everlasting destruction" (v. 9). He is now pleading with sinners to be reconciled to God through Him. Those who refuse His mercy shall stand before Him as their Judge.

5. The Kingdom Established.

Upon the ruins of the kingdoms of this present evil world will be established the Messianic kingdom. The Stone hewn out of the mountain without hands will smite the image of the Antichrist and pulverize it. When the dust thereof is scattered as the chaff on the summer threshing floor, then will appear the kingdom of the Son of man

(Dan. 2:44, 45). Christ will then reign until He has put all enemies under His feet. This is the golden age of which the wise men of all ages have dreamed and God's prophets have foretold. Peace will then fill the earth because righteousness and justice shall prevail. The knowledge of the Lord shall then cover the earth, as the waters cover the sea. Sin and sorrow shall be no more. And then, when His mediatorial work shall have been completed, He will yield the kingdom up to God, and God will become all in all (I Cor. 15:24-28). Hallelujah! Amen.